STICKER BOOK

Maurice Pledger

OCEAN WORLD!

Over 200 colorful stickers

Silver Dolphin

San Diego, California

Silver Dolphin Books

An imprint of the Advantage Publishers Group
5880 Oberlin Drive, San Diego, CA 92121-4794
www.silverdolphinbooks.com

ISBN 1-59223-222-1

Designed by Caroline Reeves
Edited by Beth Harwood and A.J. Wood

Made in Italy

1 2 3 4 5 08 07 06 05 04

About this book

Get ready to explore the ocean! Join Dewey Dolphin and his friends and find out about the many different creatures living above and below the waves.

Turn to the back of the book and you'll find lots of stickers, too. Use them to complete the sticker activities on every page by filling in the animal shapes or making your own pictures of a magnificent ocean world!

What's in the ocean?

Welcome to the ocean! Come with Dewey Dolphin on an amazing journey through the depths of the ocean, and meet many new friends along the way. Much of our planet is covered with water—and most of this water is found in our oceans, so there are lots of creatures to see.

The open ocean

Take a look over the open ocean. What can you see? Meet seabirds and sea otters, and watch for the flying fish!

Beneath the waves

Dive down beneath the waves and discover many fascinating fish. Learn how an anglerfish glows in the dark, and meet the whales.

On the seabed

Rest a while on the seabed, then venture among the rocks. Shake hands with a friendly octopus, then try to find a flatfish hiding in the sand!

Coral reef

Enter a magical underwater world. Meet some bold and beautiful creatures on the coral reef.

The edge of the ocean

Bundle up as you end your journey here in the polar regions. Find out how penguins stay warm and dry.

The open ocean

If you were sailing on the open ocean, what would you see? The ocean is full of life, from the seabirds flying above to the animals floating on the surface and the fish that swim below the waves. Here you can see a tern, a seagull, a sea otter, a huge sailfish, and some flying fish! Use your stickers to add some more creatures.

The open ocean

The open ocean is an exciting place to live! Dewey has lots of friends, including Sally Seagull and many other seabirds. Sally knows that there are thousands of ocean creatures she has never seen, as they live deep in the ocean. Use your stickers to add these creatures to the page.

Seagull

Tern

Wandering albatross

Frigate bird

Seal

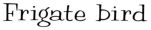

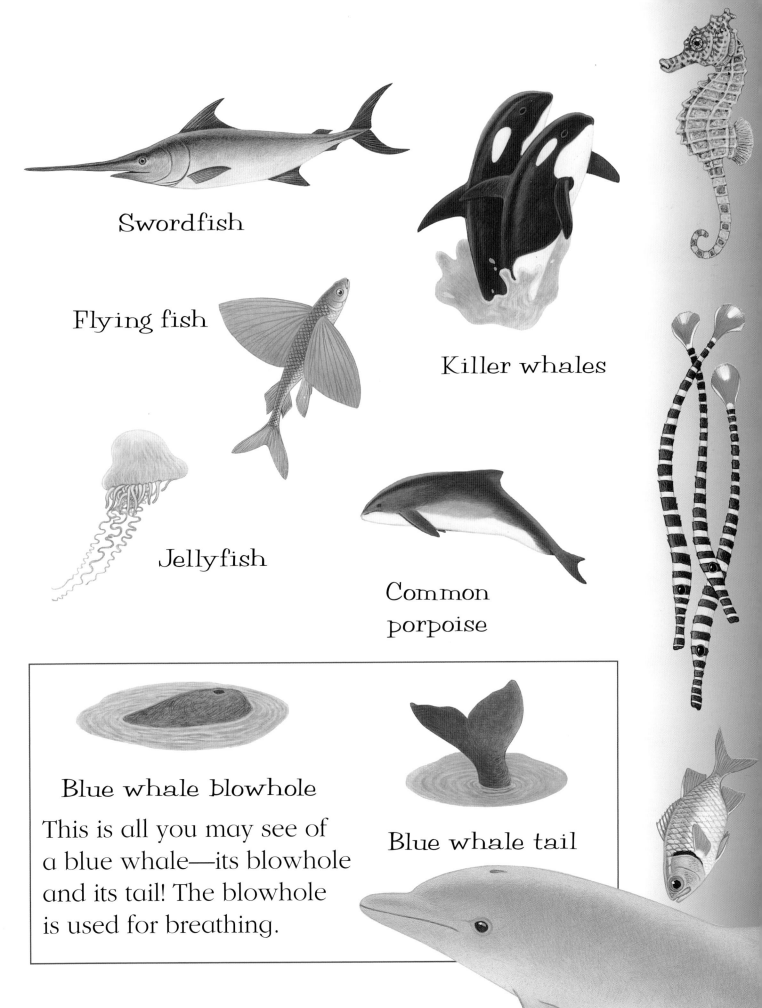

Swordfish

Flying fish

Jellyfish

Killer whales

Common porpoise

Blue whale blowhole

This is all you may see of a blue whale—its blowhole and its tail! The blowhole is used for breathing.

Blue whale tail

9

Beneath the waves

Here you are, beneath the ocean waves. Whales are the largest creatures living in the water — the biggest whale, the blue whale, can grow to be the size of a tall building! A whale is not a fish, it's a mammal, just like you. Use your stickers to add some whales to the picture.

Match the stickers
of these whales to
the pictures below.

Killer whales

Blue whale

Humpback whale

⭐ Beneath the waves

Many of Dewey Dolphin's friends are born in the ocean, but some travel from rivers to spend time in the sea, like the salmon. Did you know that the salmon can leap over other fish that get in its way? Find the right stickers on your sticker sheet to fill in the shapes. How many dolphins can you count on the opposite page? Turn the page and add more stickers to show Dewey and his friends beneath the waves.

Salmon

Mackerel

Atlantic cod

Shoal of herring

Bluefin tuna

Common bass

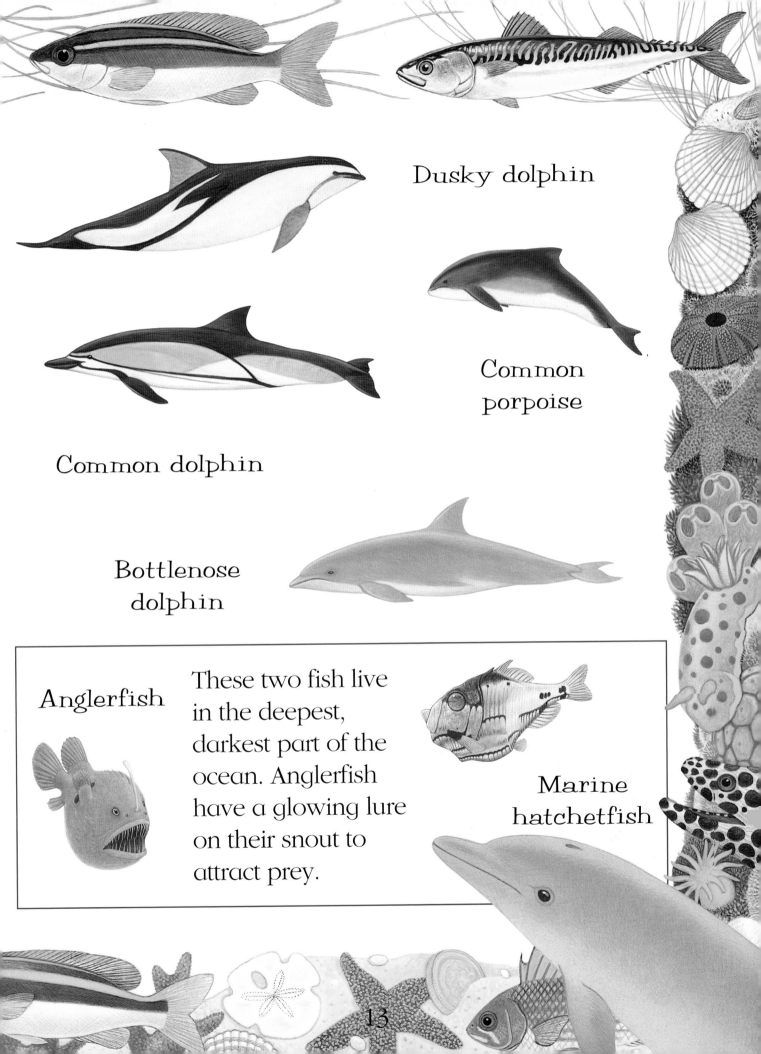

Dusky dolphin

Common porpoise

Common dolphin

Bottlenose dolphin

Anglerfish

These two fish live in the deepest, darkest part of the ocean. Anglerfish have a glowing lure on their snout to attract prey.

Marine hatchetfish

On the seabed

Dewey has some unusual friends on the seabed! Eels can squeeze in between the rocks, while crabs hide around them. Portuguese man-of-wars float through the water and have a nasty sting in their tails. Add a stingray and some seashells to the picture.

On the seabed

Here are some more of Dewey Dolphin's seabed friends. You may have to look carefully to find them because some, like plaice, hide in the sand! Others hide in shells or among the rocks. Hermit crabs make their homes in other creatures' shells. Use your stickers to fill in these pictures of Dewey's strange and amazing seabed friends. How many have you seen for yourself?

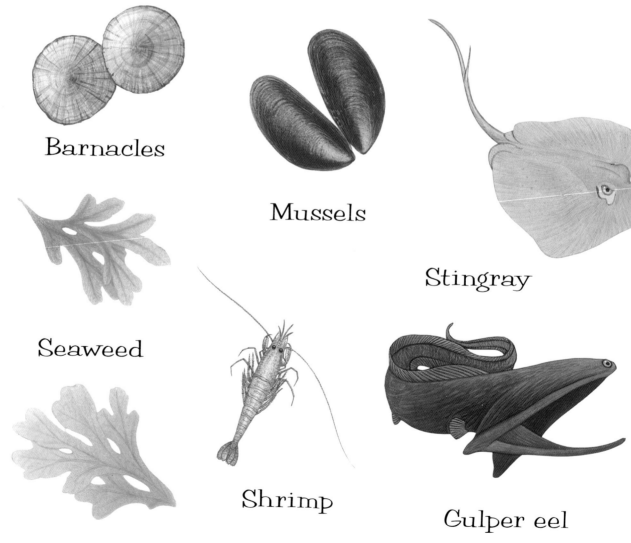

Barnacles

Mussels

Stingray

Seaweed

Shrimp

Gulper eel

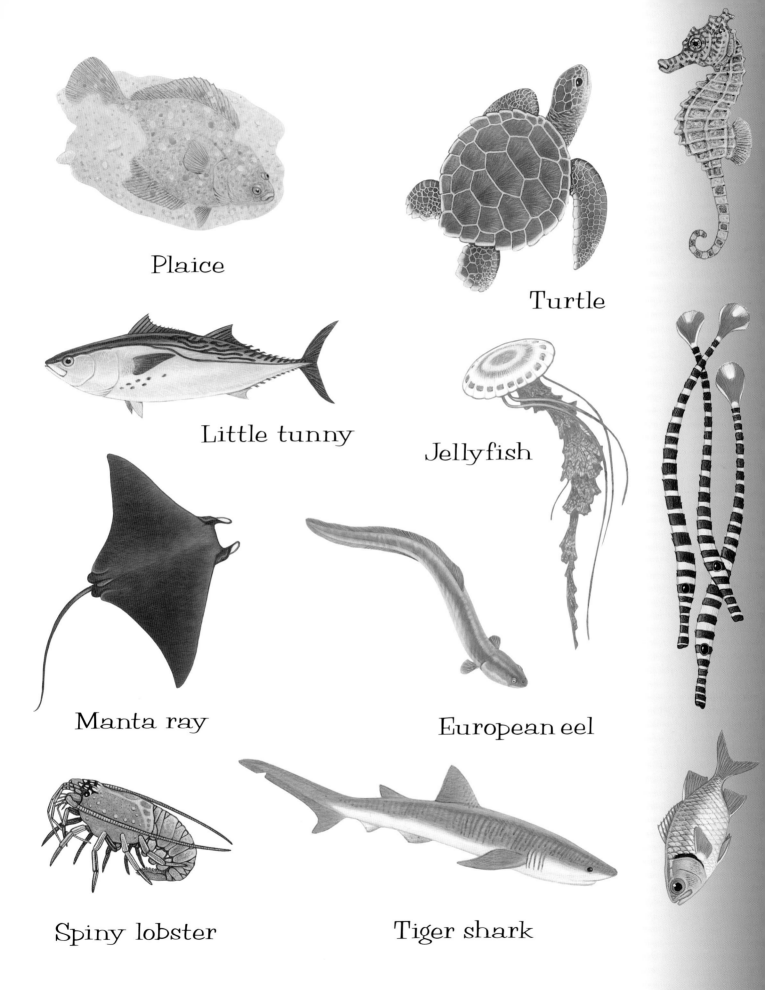

Plaice

Turtle

Little tunny

Jellyfish

Manta ray

European eel

Spiny lobster

Tiger shark

Around the rocks

Look who's here! It's Otto Octopus, welcoming
you to his underwater home. Today
he has a visitor, Brenda Butterfly
Fish. The squid and cuttlefish are
close relatives of the octopus.
They each have eight sticky arms
that help them cling to the rocks,
catch food, and swim
through the water.

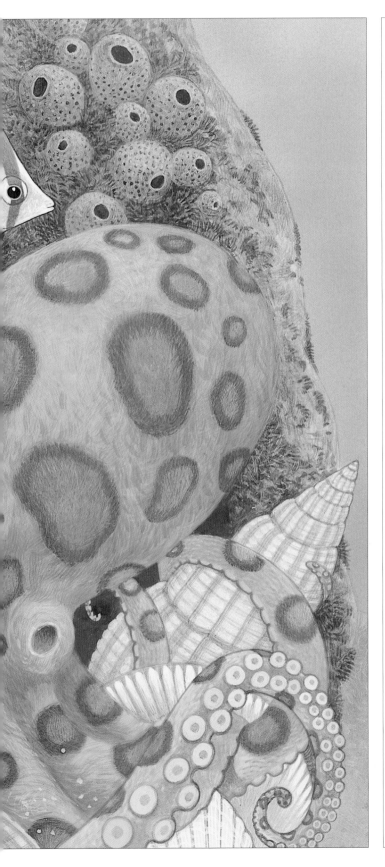

Match the right stickers from your sticker sheets to the pictures below.

Octopus

Squid

Cuttlefish

★ Around the rocks

Take a look at all the creatures you may find around the rocks or in a shallow rock pool. How many starfish and crabs can you count? Your new friend Otto Octopus is here somewhere—can you find him? These sea urchins look just like pretty stones, but they are animals, too. Now turn to your sticker pages and find the stickers to fill in the pictures.

Shells

Sea horse

Sea urchins

Crabs

Hermit crab

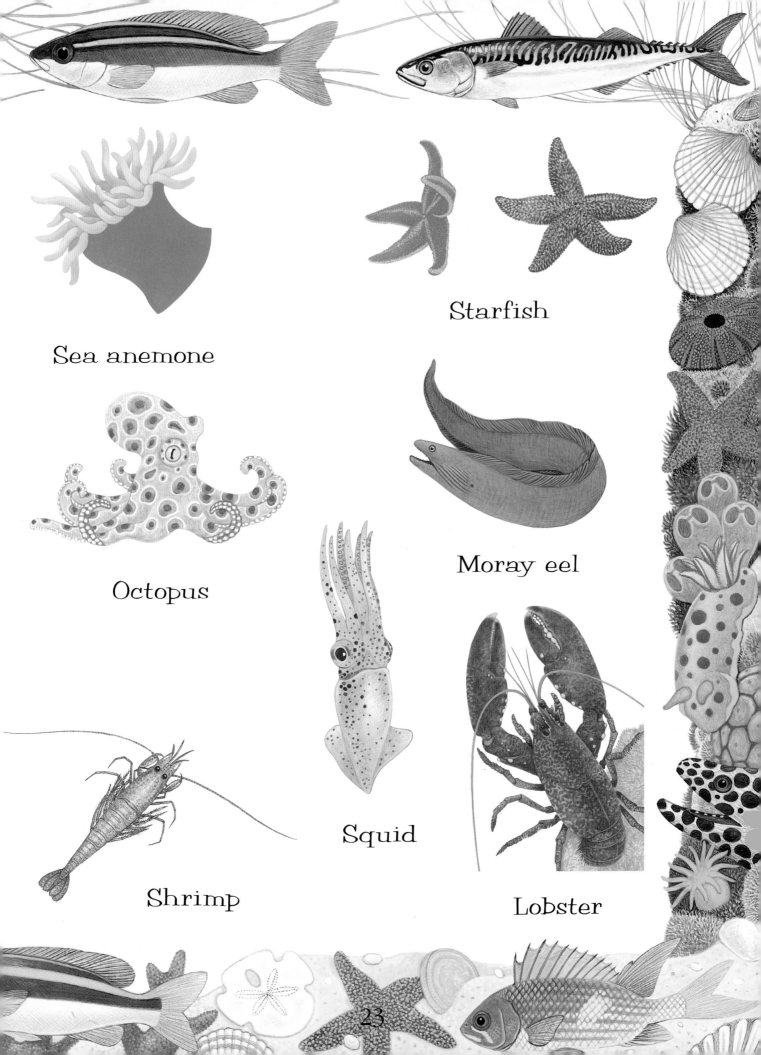

Sea anemone

Starfish

Octopus

Moray eel

Shrimp

Squid

Lobster

Shark attack!

Sharks are no more dangerous than many other creatures on our planet, but because of their huge size and their sharp teeth, they can seem very scary! Sharks have lived in oceans all over the world since the time of the dinosaurs. Did you know that the biggest shark in the world is the whale shark?

There are over 400 different types of sharks in the world. Use your stickers to show three of them!

Now
TURN THE PAGE
and make a picture of Dewey and his seabed friends.

Tiger shark

Great white shark

Hammerhead shark

Coral reef

Dewey's favorite place to explore is the beautiful coral reef, where nothing is as it seems. Can you find a striped angelfish and a red coris? Use your stickers to add three more pretty reef fish to the picture.

Coral reef

Coral reefs are found in warm, clear waters. The largest coral reef on earth is the Great Barrier Reef, off the coast of Australia, where you would find some of the amazing creatures that you see on these pages. Did you know that a gulper eel squeezes between corals and rocks, and hides with its mouth wide open, waiting for food to float in? Now use your stickers to fill in the pictures of Dewey's coral reef friends.

Sea fans

Sea pen

Sea urchin

Whelk

Abalone

Sea
cucumber

Sea slug

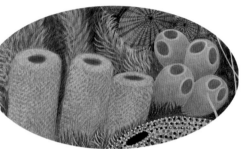

Sea squirts

Pipefish

Gulper eel

Sea
anemone

Coral

The crown-of-
thorns starfish eats
coral and destroys
coral reefs.

Crown-of-
thorns starfish

Starfish

Reef fish

Reef fish are the strangest and prettiest fish in our oceans. Look at this long, thin ribbon eel. The big blue fish is a tang—he's not afraid to be bright and bold! There's a green angelfish and a grouper here, too.

Here are some special reef fish. Find the right stickers and add them.

Clownfish hide in anemones.

Rockfish hide in the rocks.

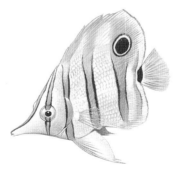

How many little blue damselfish can you count?

Butterfly fish show off their colors.

33

⭐ Reef fish

Look at all these amazing fish! Have you seen any of these in an aquarium? There are thousands of different fish living among coral reefs. Use your stickers to add all the coral reef fish you have met. Which ones do you think are the prettiest?

Reef fish

Bridled bream

Angelfish

Shadow goby

Sergeant major

Soldierfish

Redeye wrasse

Bluebanded goby

Humpnose bream

Butterfly fish

Squirrelfish

Lionfish

Spiny pufferfish

Damselfish

Reef shellfish

Shellfish are not actually fish, but are creatures that have soft bodies and a shell on their backs, like whelks or sea snails, as well as mussels, which have two shells that open up. Crabs and lobsters are also shellfish. Shellfish sometimes hide in their shells to protect themselves. Some even use their shells to help them float in the water. Help Dewey Dolphin find some of his shellfish friends by adding the right stickers to the opposite page.

Horn whelk

European cockle

Mussels

Margin shell

Nautilus

Spotted pisania

Now
TURN THE PAGE
and make your own
picture of the
coral reef.

The edge of the ocean

Welcome to the edge of the ocean! Dewey Dolphin has brought you to the polar regions, where the water is ice-cold! Walruses live near the North Pole and penguins live near the South Pole, so in real life you would never find them together!
Use your stickers to add another
penguin to the
picture.

Different kinds of creatures live near the North and South Poles.

★ The edge of the ocean

The animals that live at the edge of the ocean have to keep warm because the North and South Poles are very, very cold and icy. Walruses have a layer of fat, called blubber, under their skin that keeps them warm. Gray seals are covered with soft fur, and penguins have thick, waterproof feathers to protect them from the icy water. Find the right stickers to fill in the pictures of Dewey Dolphin's polar friends.

Arctic terns

Seagull

Wandering albatross

Emperor penguins

Cormorant

42

Gray seal

Adelie penguins

Walruses

Polar bear cub

On the shore

Your journey through the ocean is over, but the shore still waits for you, so come beachcombing with Olly Oystercatcher! When the waves drift away from the shore at low tide, they leave lots of strange things behind—what will you find? You might even uncover some buried treasure! Use your stickers to add some shells to the seashore.

Here are some of the objects you might find while beachcombing! Find the right stickers to add to the pictures.

Cockleshells

Sand dollar

Mermaid's purse

Now
TURN THE PAGE
and make a picture of
Dewey and his ocean
friends!

How to use your stickers

Look for the page numbers on the sticker sheets to help you find the right stickers for the different activities in this book. Peel each one carefully from its backing sheet and use it to fill in the shapes or add to the scenes.

You can also use your stickers to record the animals you see in real life. Look for the creatures in this book when you are near the ocean, then fill in their sticker shapes when you see them. Some animals are easier to spot than others. Some may not live where you do, so look for them when you visit an aquarium.

Enjoy your adventure through the amazing ocean world!

Add to scene on pages 6–7

Pages 8–9

Pages 10–11

Pages 12–13

Add to scene on pages 14–15

Pages 18–19

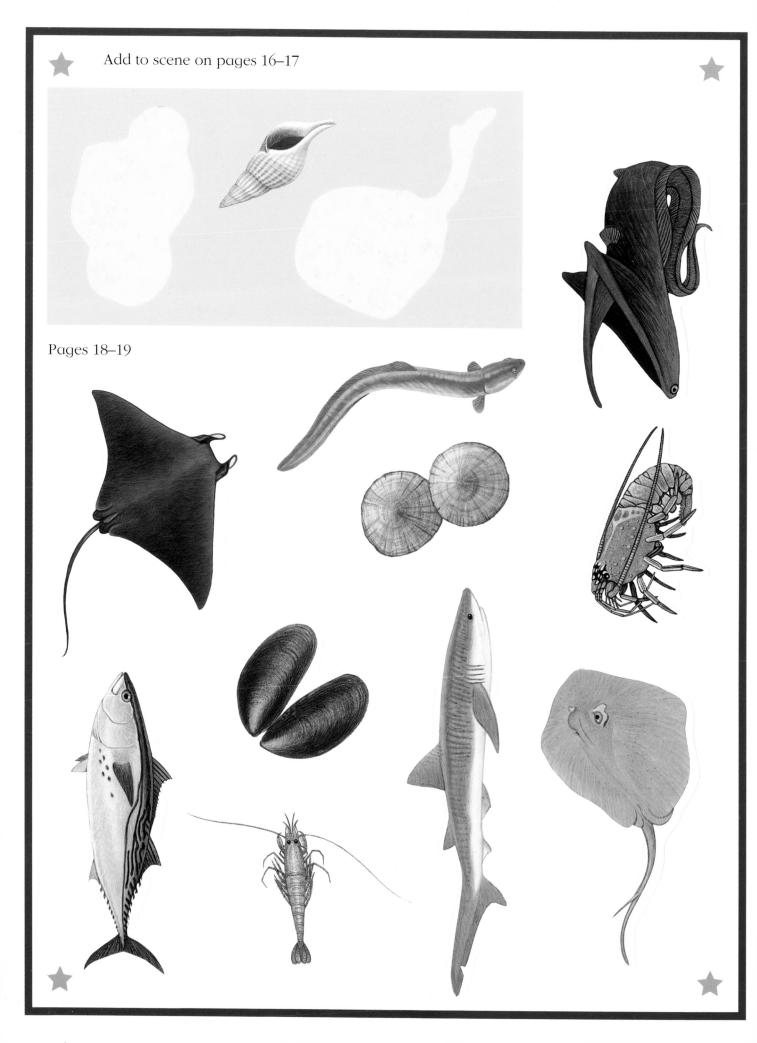

More stickers for pages 18–19

Pages 20–21

Pages 22–23

More stickers for pages 22–23

Pages 24–25

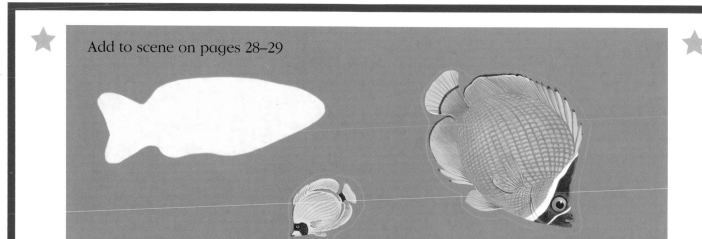

Add to scene on pages 28–29

Pages 30–31

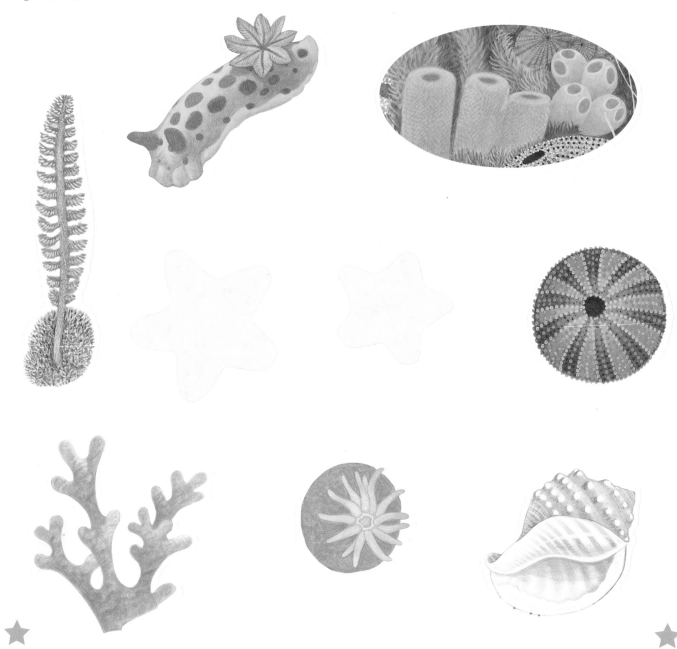

Pages 32–33

More stickers for pages 34–35

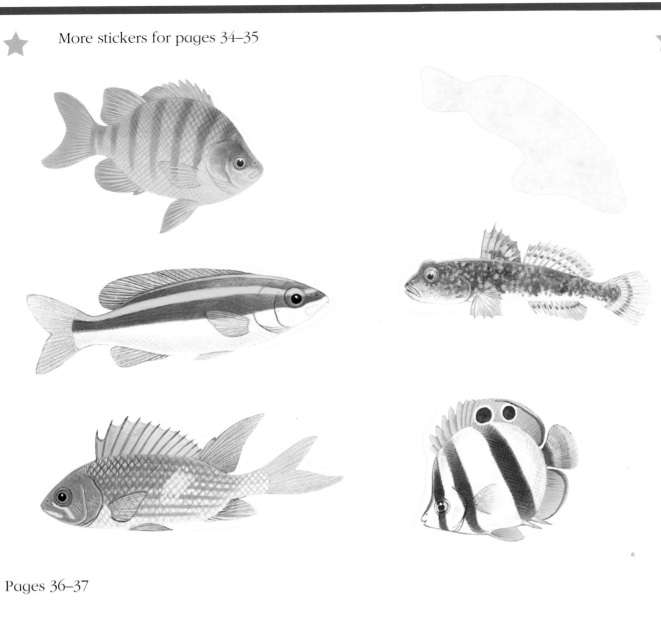

Pages 36–37

Add to scene on pages 40–41

Pages 42–43

Add to the scene on pages 46–47